SUE'S STRATEGIES®
★★★★★
Reading & Writing

BEST SPELLING CHOICES

SENSIBLE SPELLING SECRETS

BY SUSAN B. KAHN, MEd

©2019

SUE'S STRATEGIES BEST SPELLING CHOICES, SENSIBLE SPELLING SECRETS

BY SUSAN B. KAHN
SueKahnReadNow.com

ISBN 9781701543140

PRINTED IN THE UNITED STATES OF AMERICA
First printed 2019

Look for Sue's Strategies on Youtube.com

RIPPS Teaching Method
Episode 1: 2 Sounds of C
Episode 2: 2 Sounds of G
Episode 3: S as Z
Episode 4: 4 Sounds of Y
Episode 5: VCE Strategy
Episode 6: Vowel Power
Episode 7: Finding Syllables
Episode 8: Horrid R
Episode 9: Share Strategy & 3/4 Strategy
Episode10: How To Set the Vowels Free
Episode 11: Consonant LE
Episode 12: The Doubling Strategy
Episode 13: To E or Not To E
Episode 14: Consonant Y Strategy
Episode 15: CK Spelling Strategy
Episode 16: TCH Spelling Strategy
Episode 17: DGE Spelling Strategy
Episode 18: The Suffix ED Makes 3 Sounds
Episode 19: Y Before A Suffix
Episode 20: Prefixes and Suffixes
Episode 21: The Suffixes TION, SION, CIAN
Episode 22: Single U or W

TABLE OF CONTENTS: *BEST SPELLING CHOICES*

BEST SPELLING CHOICES
SENSIBLE SPELLING SECRETS

Best Spelling Choices explains numerous spelling secrets. Certain letters make more than one sound, but phonetic strategies reveal when the letter says each sound. For example, C sounds like S only if C precedes the vowels E or I or Y. All other C's produce a K sound. Look at *cir cle,* con *cert, cys* tic. The same strategy applies to the letter G. If G precedes an E or I or Y, then G sounds like J. In most other words, G will sound like the "G" in *go*. Look at sug *gest, gi gan tic, gyp sy*. Supported by these phonetic facts plus many others, a person can make more intelligent spelling choices.

Suffixes, a letter or group of letters added to the end of a root or base word, stop being so confusing when someone recognizes that suffixes are pronounced differently from the same letters as part of a real word. Certainly, a c*age* differs in meaning from leak*age*. Why not make one sound for a root word and another sound for that same group of letters as a suffix? The following suffixes sound entirely unlike their identical letters when they form a root word such as:

    IVE (dive) & IVE like invent*ive*;
    ABLE (cable) & ABLE like reason*able*;
    IBLE (bible) & IBLE like sens*ible*;
    ATE (state) & ATE like accur*ate*;
    OUS (house) & OUS like joy*ous*;
    AGE (page) & AGE like bagg*age*;
    AL (Allen) & AL like technic*al*;
    ANCE (dance) & ANCE like attend*ance*;
    ED (Ted) & ED like fixed.
Knowing suffixes improves spelling and reading accuracy.

Best Spelling Choices also makes sense by explaining various spelling strategies and their importance. To protect a vowel from losing its inside vowel sound in a root word, use the Doubling Strategy as in *runner, commend, attend*. Likewise, use the Silent E spelling strategy to protect the vowel's name, as spoken in the alphabet, in words like *late ly* and *la ter or tune ful and tu ning*.

Unfortunately, 14 percent of English words are derived from foreign languages and do not follow phonetic language patterns. Some of these words are: do, *of, was;* they must be memorized. Fortunately, most people learn these irregular words in elementary school. Therefore, knowledge of phonics and spelling strategies should result in correct spelling choices most of the time.

If a word is spelled phonetically, but the dictionary spells the word differently, a spell-checker may assist with such minor corrections. For example, beaf is not the right way to spell roast beef, but a spell checker could fix this type of phonetic error. However, without phonetic input, the spell-checker may be too confused to repair the spelling. Knowing phonics helps.

When spelling an unknown word, follow this procedure: (1) say each syllable out loud; (2) write the sounds heard 1 syllable at a time; (3) read the completed word orally in syllables to be sure all the needed sounds are positioned in the right places. This process should increase self confidence in expressing ideas in writing and should decrease anxiety about writing. Try these strategies; you will like them!

Susan B. Kahn

WHAT IS A SYLLABLE?

A SYLLABLE MAKES 1 AND ONLY 1 VOWEL SOUND.

SIZE VARIES FROM 1 TO 6 LETTERS.

EXAMPLES: <u>A</u>, SW<u>I</u>TCH, N<u>O</u>TE, F<u>UR</u>, TI <u>TLE</u>, P<u>EA</u>CE

THE 6 VOWELS ARE: A, E, I, O, U, Y

LETTERS MAY COMBINE TO CREATE ONLY 1 VOWEL SOUND.

EACH OF THE 6 SYLLABLE TYPES PRODUCES A SPECIAL VOWEL SOUND.

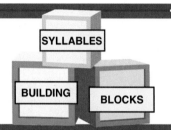

IF 1 VOWEL IS LAST, IT SAYS ITS NAME WITH A BLAST.

EXAMPLES:
SOLO & EMU
S<u>O</u> L<u>O</u> & <u>E</u> M<u>U</u>

IF 1 VOWEL COMES INSIDE 1 OR MORE CONSONANTS, A DIFFERENT SOUND IS HEARD.

EXAMPLES:
D<u>A</u>N & B<u>E</u>TH

IN A 1 VOWEL, 1 CONSONANT, 1 ENDING SILENT E SYLLABLE, THE FIRST VOWEL SAYS ITS NAME.

EXAMPLES:
J<u>U</u>NE & D<u>A</u>VE

IF 1 VOWEL PRECEDES THE LETTER R, THESE 2 LETTERS COMBINE TO MAKE AN ER SOUND MOSTLY.

EXAMPLE: B<u>UR</u> GL<u>AR</u>

A 3 LETTER, ENDING CONSONANT LE SYLLABLE SEPARATES.

EXAMPLES:
RID <u>DLE</u> & CA <u>BLE</u>

SOMETIMES, VOWELS JOIN TO FORM 1 SOUND:
EA IN R<u>EA</u>D; OO IN B<u>OO</u>K
SOMETIMES, CONSONANTS JOIN VOWELS TO CREATE 1 VOWEL:
OW IN SN<u>OW</u>; AY IN D<u>AY.</u>

SYLLABLES COMBINE TO BUILD MULTI-SYLLABIC WORDS.

EACH VOWEL CAN MAKE 3 SOUNDS.

USE **POSITION** TO CHOOSE THE RIGHT SOUND.

WHEN ONE VOWEL COMES LAST,
IT SAYS ITS NAME WITH A BLAST.

A LAST	E LAST	I LAST
JA COB	WE	BRI AN
JA SON	PE TER	I RENE
FA BLE	RE PAY	PI LOT

$$

O LAST	U LAST	Y LAST
GRO VER	JU LIE	*IF 1 SYLLABLE*
JO SEPH	SU SAN	DRY
PO TA TO	MU SE UM	SPY
		RY AN

"LAST" MEANS THE FINAL LETTER IN ANY SYLLABLE.
"NAME" MEANS THE LETTER'S NAME IN THE ALPHABET.
A VOWEL THAT IS LAST SYLLABLE MAY STAND ALONE OR
COMBINE WITH OTHER SYLLABLES: A, DE LAY for delay,
COM PRO MISE for compromise, E MO TION for emotion.

EACH VOWEL CAN MAKE 3 SOUNDS.

USE POSITION TO CHOOSE THE RIGHT SOUND.

WHEN A CONSONANT ENDS THE WORD, A DIFFERENT VOWEL SOUND IS HEARD.

A INSIDE
AL
PASS
CATCH

E INSIDE
HEN
EGGS
MELTS

I INSIDE
IT
PIGS
TWITCH

O INSIDE
ON
LONG
SOCKS

U INSIDE
RUN
DUMP
LUNCH

Y INSIDE
MYTH
SYNTH
CYM BAL

WHEN 1 VOWEL COMES BEFORE 1 OR MORE ENDING CONSONANTS, THEN A DIFFERENT VOWEL SOUND IS HEARD. THESE INSIDE SYLLABLES COMBINE WITH OTHER SYLLABLES: EN TER TAIN, IN SPIRE, COM PRE HEN SION.

WHICH U SOUND IS THE RIGHT ONE?

WHEN **U** IS NOT LAST, IT MAKES THE SOUND HEARD IN: THE P<u>U</u>PPY SITS <u>U</u>P.

PUPPY

J<u>U</u>ST DRIVE THE B<u>U</u>S & PICK <u>US</u> UP.

PU PIL

MU SEUM

WHEN **U** IS LAST, IT MAY SOUND LIKE ITS LETTER NAME IN THE ALPHABET: P<u>U</u> PIL, M<u>U</u> SEUM.

THE <u>U</u> NICORN FROM <u>U</u> TAH AM<u>U</u> SES THE CROWD.

STU DENT

E MU

SOMETIMES THE **U** WHICH ENDS THE SYLLABLE MAY SOUND LIKE THE **OO** IN MOON: ST<u>U</u> DENT, E M<u>U</u>

S<u>U</u> SAN & J<u>U</u> LIE BECAME ILL WITH THE FL<u>U</u>.

MULE

JUNE

VOWEL - CONSONANT - E SYLLABLES WITH **U** ALSO MAKE BOTH **U** SOUNDS.

BUILD WORDS 1 SYLLABLE AT A TIME WITH THE SUFFIX **TION** (which sounds like SHUN)	HOW? SAY EACH SYLLABLE. SPELL EACH SYLLABLE. ADD THE SUFFIX, **TION**

TION COMBINES WITH A SYLLABLE TYPE THAT <u>ENDS</u> WITH ONLY **1** VOWEL.

VA	CA	TION
DE	LE	TION
CI	TA	TION
PRO	MO	TION
MU	TA	TION

TION COMBINES WITH A SYLLABLE TYPE THAT KEEPS ITS **1** SINGLE VOWEL <u>INSIDE</u> **1** OR MORE CONSONANTS.

AT	TEN	TION
EX	CEP	TION
IN	FEC	TION
CON	VEN	TION
SUB	TRAC	TION

MIX AND MATCH: COMBINE INSIDE SYLLABLES PLUS VOWEL IS LAST SYLLABLES IN ANY ORDER BEFORE THE SUFFIX, **TION**.

SEN	SA	TION
PRE	DIC	TION
IN	FEC	TION
PRO	DUC	TION
FRUS	TRA	TION

BUILD SOME LONGER WORDS!

*SAY EACH SYLLABLE.
*SPELL EACH SYLLABLE.
*READ THAT SYLLABLE TO MAKE SURE IT IS CORRECT.

LO	CO	MO	TION
IN	SU	LA	TION
AP	PRO	BA	TION
REP	U	TA	TION
COM	MEN	DA	TION

THE VOWEL CONSONANT E ENDING SYLLABLE

1 Vowel, 1 Consonant, 1 E, an ending group of 3!

Silent E forces the other vowel
to say its name alphabetically.
The 1st vowel may vary;
The Consonant between the vowels may vary.

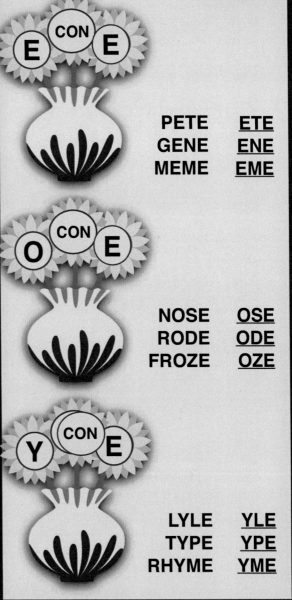

A CON E		E CON E	
SALE	ALE	PETE	ETE
SPADE	ADE	GENE	ENE
TRACE	ACE	MEME	EME

I CON E		O CON E	
NICE	ICE	NOSE	OSE
MINE	INE	RODE	ODE
WIDE	IDE	FROZE	OZE

U CON E		Y CON E	
TUNE	UNE	LYLE	YLE
HUGE	UGE	TYPE	YPE
BRUTE	UTE	RHYME	YME

BUILD WORDS
1 SYLLABLE AT A TIME
WITH 1 VOWEL,
1 CONSONANT,
1 ENDING SILENT E.

HOW
SAY EACH SYLLABLE.
SPELL EACH SYLLABLE.
READ THE SYLLABLES
ORALLY TO PROOFREAD.

DO	NATE
DE	PLETE
RE	VISE
PRO	POSE
A	CUTE
RE	STYLE

VCE COMBINES WITH A VOWEL IS LAST SYLLABLE.

MIS	PLACE
COM	PETE
AD	VISE
SUP	POSE
IM	MUNE
EN	ZYME

VCE COMBINES WITH AN INSIDE VOWEL SYLLABLE.

AD	VO	CATE
RE	CON	VENE
IM	PRO	VISE
PRE	DIS	POSE
AB	SO	LUTE
GIG	A	BYTE

MIX AND MATCH:
COMBINE INSIDE SYLLABLES PLUS VOWEL IS LAST SYLLABLES IN ANY ORDER BEFORE THE **VCE** SYLLABLE.

BUILD SOME LONGER WORDS!

✦ SAY EACH SYLLABLE.
✦ SPELL THAT SYLLABLE.
✦ READ THE WHOLE WORD TO MAKE SURE IT IS CORRECT.

IN	VES	TI	GATE
AC	CU	MU	LATE
PER	SU	ADE	

THE SHARE STRATEGY

IF **2** OR **4** CONSONANTS STAND BETWEEN **2** SPOKEN VOWEL SOUNDS, SHARE THE CONSONANTS EQUALLY.

1) Underline the vowel sounds.
2) Share the consonants equally between the vowel sounds.

1	1
DEB	BY
GYM	NAST
UN	LIKE

2	2
HAND	STAND
DIPH	THONG
MILK	SHAKE

IF **3** CONSONANTS COME BETWEEN **2** VOWEL SOUNDS, PLACE **1** CONSONANT ON THE LEFT AND **2** CONSONANTS ON THE RIGHT MOST OF THE TIME.

1	2
MIS	TRUST
DIS	PLAY
EX	CLUDE

THE SHARE STRATEGY WORKS ON EVEN LARGER WORDS:

IN VEN TED,   OB JEC TING,   PER MIS SION

TO UNDERSTAND AND APPLY SPELLING STRATEGIES, YOU NEED TO **KNOW** THE **SHARE** AND 3/4 **STRATEGIES** FOR SYLLABICATION. ONLY THEN WILL YOU BE ABLE TO READ & CORRECT YOUR ERRORS.

THE **3/4** STRATEGY

IF ONLY **1** CONSONANT STANDS BETWEEN **2** SPOKEN VOWEL SOUNDS, A SHARE CAN'T BE DONE!

1	2
3	4

1) UNDERLINE THE VOWEL SOUNDS.
2) KEEP THE **1** VOWEL SOUND LAST.
3) PUSH THE **1** CONSONANT TO THE RIGHT **3** OUT OF **4** TIMES.

E	LI
LA	BEL
TEA	CHER

I	TEM
O	PEN
U	NITE

THE 3/4 STRATEGY WORKS ON EVEN LARGER WORDS:

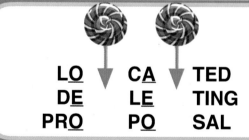

LO	CA	TED
DE	LE	TING
PRO	PO	SAL

MANY WORDS COMBINE THE SHARE STRATEGY AND THE 3/4 STRATEGY.

	COM	PO	SER	COMPOSER
	EX	TRO	VERT	EXTROVERT
RE	CIP	RO	CATE	RECIPROCATE
PRE	SEN	TA	TION	PRESENTATION

CHOICES FOR SPELLING THE K SOUND:

C, K, CK, CH

CHOOSE **C** WHENEVER POSSIBLE! IT'S THE BEST CHOICE!

CLARA ENJOYS A CUPCAKE WITH WHIPPED CREAM AND CANDY. SHE DOES NOT EAT CUCUMBERS.

USE **K** WHEN **C** SOUNDS LIKE **S**.
C BEFORE THE VOWELS **E, I,** & **Y**
MAKES AN **S** SOUND.

KETTLE

CETTLE
NOT A WORD

KITE

CITE
PRONOUNCED SITE

KYLE

CYLE
NOT A WORD

MEMORY TRICK FOR CE, CI, CY:
OLD MCDONALD GREW A SMART TREE; E, I, E, I, Y.

CHOOSE **CK** ONLY IF:
CK ENDS A **1** SYLLABLE WORD
AND **CK** FOLLOWS ONLY **1** VOWEL.

CHECK TO SEE IF MY PACKAGE HAS ARRIVED. PICK IT UP.
* A **CK** WORD MAY ADD A SUFFIX LIKE *AGE* IN PACKAGE.

CHOOSE **CH** TO SPELL THE **K** SOUND
IN WORDS DERIVED FROM THE GREEK
LANGUAGE SUCH AS:
CHRISTMAS, CHORUS, CHORD.

CHOICES FOR SPELLING THE J SOUND: GE, GI, GY, DGE, J.

CHOOSE G TO MAKE A J SOUND

BEFORE THE VOWELS E OR I OR Y.

GEORGY AND GINGER WORKED IN THE GARAGE.
GINA PRACTICES GYPSY SONGS IN THE GYM.

MEMORY TRICK FOR GE, GI, GY:
OLD MCDONALD GREW A SMART TREE: E, I, E, I, Y.

G MAKES A HARD SOUND LIKE THE G IN "GO"
BEFORE ALL OTHER LETTERS:

GLEN WILL GO TO THE GAME WITH GLORIA,
AND THEY WILL GULP DRINKS.

CHOOSE J TO MAKE A J SOUND:

JOE, JACK, AND JUDY JUMP FOR JOY
WHEN THEIR TEAM WON.

TRY READING ALL THESE J WORDS WITH THE G SOUND
FROM "GO." THESE WORDS WILL SOUND QUITE SILLY

SO THE LETTER J WAS NEEDED.

CHOOSE DGE.

DGE SPELLS WORDS IF:
DGE ENDS A 1 SYLLABLE WORD
& DGE FOLLOWS ONLY 1 VOWEL.

BADGE, EDGE, BRIDGE,
DODGE, FUDGE

CHOOSE GE TO CREATE THE J SOUND.

FRIENDS DISCOURAGE
GEORGE & GINGER FROM
SEEKING REVENGE.

CHOICES

CK or K?   **TCH or CH?**   **DGE or GE?**

CHOOSE THE LONGER SPELLING TO END **1** SYLLABLE
WORDS, IF THE ENDING FOLLOWS ONLY **1** VOWEL.

ARE CK, TCH, & DGE ACTING LIKE
SPOILED, DEMANDING LETTERS?
THEN THE WI**TCH** MAY KICK
THEM OFF THE BRI**DGE**?

CK
SA**CK**
SPE**CK**
SI**CK**
SO**CK**
SU**CK**

TCH
BA**TCH**
SKE**TCH**
STI**TCH**
BO**TCH**
BU**TCH**

DGE
BA**DGE**
LE**DGE**
FRI**DGE**
LO**DGE**
FU**DGE**

CK, TCH, DGE DO NOT SPELL WORDS WITH **2** *VOWELS.*

C**OO**K
S**EE**K
W**EA**K

BL**EA**CH
L**EE**CH
GR**OU**CH

L**IE**GE
SCR**OO**GE
R**OU**GE

*CK, TCH, DGE DO NOT SPELL WORDS IF AN INTERFERING
CONSONANT PRECEDES THEM. THEN K, CH, GE ARE USED.*

RA**N**K
PA**R**K
WO**R**K

PI**N**CH
SCO**R**CH
STA**R**CH

PU**R**GE
CRI**N**GE
LA**R**GE

WORDS ENDING IN CK, TCH, DGE MAY ADD SUFFIXES:

BLOCK*AGE*   PITCH*ER*   LODG*ED*
SOCK*ET*   ETCH*ING*   LEDGE*S*

SPELLING PRACTICE FOR CK, TCH, DGE
CHOOSE THE CORRECT ENDING FOR EACH WORD.

CK OR K?	TCH OR CH?	DGE OR GE?
CLI____	CLU____	PLE____
SEE ____	SNA ____	WA___E
MIL____	WI____	MAR____
LO____	SKE____	DRE____
STA____	PEA____	BA____
TRUN____	PER____	FOR____
DE____	POR____	DIR____
STOR____	LUN____	JU____
SIL___	BIR____	MER____
STU____	MAR____	BRI____
PAR____	BEA____	CHAR____
PU____	BU____	LO____
TRA____	DU____	PUR____
WOR____	TOR ____	BAR____
KI____	MI____	E____

A VOWEL, CONSONANT, ENDING SILENT E SYLLABLE NEVER USES DGE.

SPELLING PRACTICE FOR CK, TCH, DGE
CHOOSE THE CORRECT ENDING FOR EACH WORD.

CK OR K?	TCH OR CH?	DGE OR GE?
BLEA___	LAUN____	BUD____
FLI_____	POU _____	LE____
TI_____	REA____	SCROO_____
KNO____	FREN____	FU_____
HI__E	CRU_____	FRIN___
SNU____	SWI_____	SMI____
CRA___	NO____	OBLI_____E
HOO__	STRE____	RI____
FOR__	AR_____	HU___E
RA___E	HA____	SPLUR_____
HAW___	BEN___	WE_____
SMIR_____	DREN____	ORAN_____
STAR____	IN____	STA___E
WEE____	REA____	SLU_____
THI____	BA_____	LAR_____

A VOWEL, CONSONANT, ENDING SILENT E SYLLABLE NEVER USES DGE.

CHOICE: S OR Z TO MAKE THE SOUND OF Z

THE LETTER Z USUALLY BEGINS OR ENDS WORDS.

BEGINNING Z

ZEBRA
ZERO
ZIPPER
ZOO

ENDING Z

JAZZ
FIZZ
BUZZ
QUIZ

ENDING ZE

SIZE
SEIZE
SNEEZE
FREEZE

USE S BETWEEN 2 VOWELS TO MAKE A Z SOUND MOST OF THE TIME.

VOWEL
S
VOWEL

VSV = Z

ILLUSION: SUSAN FINDS WRITING PROSE EASY.
DECISION: WILL RON CHOOSE A DIESEL OR ELECTRIC CAR?
CONFUSION: THE HOLIDAY SEASON CAUSED THE TRAFFIC JAM.

SOME COMMON EXCEPTIONS ARE:

AS, DOES, HAS, IS, SAYS WAS.

THE ENDING S CREATES A Z SOUND.

WAS THE DRIVER GUILTY? HE *SAYS* HE *IS* INNOCENT.
DOES ANYONE BELIEVE HIM IF HE *HAS* DRIVEN
THROUGH A RED LIGHT *AS* IF DRUNK?

ENDING A OR AY: WHICH DO YOU CHOOSE?

ENDING A SOUNDS LIKE THE A IN AMERICA.

ANNA LIVES IN AFRICA.
EMMA LIVES IN INDIA.
CARLA LIVES IN CHINA.
LAURA LIVES IN CANADA.

21 STATES IN THE U.S. END IN A:

AMERICA

ALASKA, ALABAMA, ARIZONA, CALIFORNIA, FLORIDA, GEORGIA, IOWA, INDIANA, LOUISIANA, MINNESOTA, MONTANA, NEBRASKA, NEVADA, NORTH & SOUTH CAROLINA, NORTH & SOUTH DAKOTA, OKLAHOMA, PENNSYLVANIA, VIRGINIA & WEST VIRGINIA.

HOW DO YOU SPELL A, THE FIRST LETTER IN THE ALPHABET, AT THE END OF A WORD? AY!

RAY MUST DELAY HIS TRIP UNTIL FRIDAY.
FAY WILL RELAY THIS MESSAGE TODAY.

DAYS OF WEEK

MONDAY
TUESDAY
WEDNESDAY
THURSDAY
FRIDAY
SATURDAY
SUNDAY

OCTOBER

S	M	T	W	T	F	S
		1	2	3	4	5
6	7	8	9	10	11	12
13	14	15	16	17	18	19
20	21	22	23	24	25	26
27	28	29	30	31		

CHOICE: E OR Y AT THE END OF A WORD?

WHAT SOUND DOES ENDING E MAKE?
NONE!
ENDING E IS SILENT IN ALMOST ALL WORDS.

DAVE MAKES A CHOICE TO SOLVE THE PUZZLE ABOUT A LARGE THEFT OF PAINTINGS.

DAVE & MAKE - ENDING SILENT E CAUSES THE PRECEDING VOWEL TO SAY ITS NAME AS BOTH WORDS EXEMPLIFY THE 1 VOWEL, 1 CONSONANT, 1 SILENT E SYLLABLE.

CHOICE - ENDING SILENT E CHANGES THE SOUND OF C TO S.

SOLVE - ENDING SILENT E FOLLOWS WORDS ENDING IN V.

PUZZLE - ENDING SILENT E COMPLETES THE 3 LETTER ENDING SYLLABLE, **CONSONANT LE.**

LARGE - ENDING SILENT E CHANGES THE SOUND OF G TO J.

THE MANY USES OF Y AT ENDS OF WORDS

Y
CY
LY
TY
ITY
ARY
ORY
OLOGY

DEBBY BOUGHT AN IVY PLANT FOR TEDDY WHOSE INJURY CREATED A POSSIBLE EMERGENCY.

FORTUNATELY, LABORATORY TESTS SHOW THAT TEDDY WILL MAKE A SPEEDY RECOVERY.

STUDYING BIOLOGY PLUS NECESSARY TESTS REVEAL THE IDENTITY OF A NEW SAFETY PROCEDURE.

CHOICE: I OR Y AT THE END OF A WORD?

IF ONLY A FEW WORDS END IN I AND MAKE THE I SOUND,
HOW DO YOU SPELL ENDING I?

Y !

SOME WORDS THAT END WITH I ARE:
HI,   RABBI,   I

THE ENDING VOWEL Y MAKES THE I SOUND
FOR 3 GROUPS OF WORDS
PLUS SOME OTHERS:

GROUP 1	Y SAYS I AT THE END OF ONE SYLLABLE WORDS LIKE: BY, CRY, SPY.
GROUP 2	Y SAYS I AS PART OF THE SUFFIX, FY: MYSTIFY, TERRIFY, SIMPLIFY.
GROUP 1	Y SAYS I AS PART OF THE ROOT, PLY: APPLY, REPLY, SUPPLY.
OTHERS	WORDS ALSO USING ENDING Y FOR I: DENY, ALLY, RELY,

CONCLUSION: USE Y TO SPELL THE VOWELS
A, E, & I
AT THE VERY, VERY ENDS OF WORDS.

AY = A WHEN LAST	Y = E WHEN LAST	Y = I WHEN LAST
CLAY	SUNNY	MY
SPRAY	DYNASTY	COMPLY
SUNDAY	SYMPHONY	SIGNIIFY

CHOICE: DOES A WORD END WITH O OR OW?

BOTH O AND OW MAKE AN O SOUND AT THE END OF A WORD. WHICH DO YOU CHOOSE?

OW OW OFTEN ENDS 1 SYLLABLE WORDS WITH ONLY 1 VOWEL SOUND LIKE:

BOW, BLOW, CROW, FLOW, GLOW, LOW, MOW, KNOW, ROW, SHOW, SLOW, SNOW, TOW.

SOME LARGER WORDS ALSO END IN OW:

ARROW, BELOW, FELLOW, MINNOW, SHADOW, SWALLOW, WINDOW, YELLOW, MARSHMALLOW, TOMORROW

O

SOME LONGER, FOREIGN BASED WORDS END IN O LIKE:

LIBRETTO, POLITICO, <u>SOMBRERO</u>, ALFRESCO, CONCERTO, STACCATO, ESPRESSO.

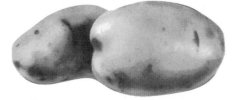

SOME OTHER WORDS ALSO PREFER O AT THE END:

EGO, AGO, BIO, HERO, SOLO, ALSO, ZERO, TYPO, CELLO, POTATO, TOMATO, ROMEO, RODEO,

WHAT IS A SUFFIX?

A SUFFIX, A LETTER OR GROUP OF LETTERS, FOLLOWS A ROOT WORD OR A LATIN OR GREEK ROOT.

SUFFIX

THE SING<u>ING</u> IS RING<u>ING</u> IN MY EARS.   *IS ING A SUFFIX?*   YES

TAKE THE LUGG<u>AGE</u> TO THE COTT<u>AGE</u>.   *IS AGE A SUFFIX?*   YES

WE CYCL<u>ED</u> ON RENT<u>ED</u> BIKES.   *IS ED A SUFFIX?*   YES

STRATEGY: TRY REMOVING THE SUFFIX.
DOES A REAL WORD REMAIN?
A REAL WORD MUST REMAIN
FOR THE LETTERS TO BE CONSIDERED A SUFFIX.

S<u>ING</u>   *IS ING A SUFFIX?*   NO

ST<u>AGE</u>   *IS AGE A SUFFIX?*   NO

FL<u>ED</u>   *IS ED A SUFFIX?*   NO

A SUFFIX FOLLOWS A WORD OR ROOT UNLESS A SECOND SUFFIX FOLLOWS THE FIRST SUFFIX TO END THE WORD: CARE<u>FUL</u>, CAREFUL<u>LY</u>;   VI<u>SION</u>, VISION<u>ARY</u>

A SUFFIX CAN CHANGE
THE SYNTAX OF A WORD:

VERB INTO NOUN - CREATE TO CREATION;

VERB INTO ADJECTIVE - CREATE TO CREATIVE.

THE DOUBLING STRATEGY

PP TT GG

TA**PP**ING & TA**P**ING HAVE DIFFERENT MEANINGS!

**DOUBLING A CONSONANT
PROTECTS & SAVES AN INSIDE VOWEL'S SOUND
BY ADDING A TWIN CONSONANT.
DOUBLING MAY BE NEEDED AT THE BEGINNING,
MIDDLE, OR END OF A WORD BUT NOT TOO OFTEN.**

**TO UNDERSTAND <u>WHEN</u> TO USE THE DOUBLING STRATEGY,
YOU NEED TO KNOW THE SOUND A SINGLE VOWEL MAKES:**

1) **A SINGLE VOWEL THAT ENDS A SYLLABLE SAYS ITS NAME
   IN THE ALPHABET LIKE *HI, RO ME O*.**

2) **A SINGLE VOWEL THAT IS FOLLOWED BY 1 OR MORE
   CONSONANTS WILL MAKE A SHORT VOWEL SOUND LIKE
   DEB AND DAN SPRINT TO CATCH THE BUS.**

**YOU ALSO NEED TO KNOW WHICH LETTERS BELONG IN A
SYLLABLE TO FIGURE OUT THE CORRECT VOWEL SOUND.
HERE ARE THE RULES FOR SYLLABICATION:**

**IF 2 OR MORE CONSONANTS
COME BETWEEN TWO VOWEL SOUNDS,
SHARE THE CONSONANTS AS EQUALLY AS POSSIBLE.
EXAMPLES: *WIN* NING MAKES KIDS *HAP PY*.**

**IF ONLY 1 CONSONANT COMES BETWEEN 2 VOWEL SOUNDS,
KEEP THE VOWEL LAST AND PUSH THE CONSONANT
TO THE NEXT SYLLABLE
3/4 OF THE TIME.**

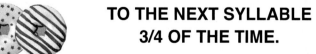

EXAMPLES: PE TER AND DA VID DE VOUR DO NUTS.

DOUBLING STRATEGY — PART 1

MOST WORDS DO NOT NEED TO DOUBLE A CONSONANT.

3 REASONS FOR NOT DOUBLING:

1: A ROOT WORD WITH **2** ENDING CONSONANTS WILL <u>NOT</u> <u>DOUBLE</u> EITHER OF THEM.

LA<u>ST</u> & ED	LAS | TED
STA<u>RT</u> & ED	STAR | TED
BA<u>ND</u> & ED	BAN | DED

AN ENDING CONSONANT WITH A BUDDY SHARES ONE ENDING CONSONANT WITH A SUFFIX. THE INSIDE VOWEL IS STILL PROTECTED.

2: A WORD WITH A **2** LETTER VOWEL TEAM WILL <u>NOT</u> <u>DOUBLE</u> ITS ENDING CONSONANT.

R<u>AI</u>N & Y = RAINY
SN<u>OW</u> & Y = SNOWY
SL<u>EE</u>P & Y = SLEEPY

A VOWEL WITH A BUDDY ALWAYS KEEPS ITS OWN SOUND.

3: A WORD WITH **1** VOWEL & **1** ENDING CONSONANT WILL <u>NOT</u> <u>DOUBLE</u> ITS ENDING CONSONANT <u>IF</u> THE SUFFIX BEGINS WITH A CONSONANT.

DIM & <u>LY</u> = DIMLY
SIN & <u>FUL</u> = SINFUL
SAD & <u>NESS</u> = SADNESS

IF A SUFFIX THAT BEGINS WITH A CONSONANT JOINS AN AT RISK WORD, *1 WHICH HAS ONLY 1 VOWEL AND ONLY 1 ENDING CONSONANT,* THE VOWEL SOUND IN THE ROOT WORD IS PROTECTED BY KEEPING ITS OWN ENDING CONSONANT.

DOUBLING STRATEGY PART 2

WHEN TO DOUBLE!
ONLY SOME WORDS NEED A TWIN CONSONANT.

1: AN INSIDE VOWEL CAN KEEP ITS SOUND **IF** A TWIN CONSONANT IS FOUND AND ADDED BEFORE THE SUFFIX.

WIN & ER	WIN	NER	**WITHOUT A TWIN,**
TAP & ED	TAP	PED	**THE SINGLE VOWEL**
FIT & ING	FIT	TING	**WOULD SAY ITS NAME**
			IN THE ALPHABET:

WI NER   TA PED   FI TING

2: ADDING A TWIN LETTER WITHIN A WORD PROTECTS 1 VOWEL SO ITS REAL SOUND IS HEARD.

<u>YES</u>!		<u>NO</u>!	
A<u>TT</u>END	A	TEND	**A VOWEL WITHOUT A BUDDY**
A<u>SS</u>IST	A	SIST	**MAY NEED A TWIN**
SU<u>GG</u>EST	SU	GEST	**TO SPELL BETTER.**
CO<u>MM</u>AND	CO	MAND	

3: ADDING A TWIN LETTER BEFORE THE SUFFIX MAY BE NEEDED IN SOME MULTISYLLABIC WORDS IF:

THE SYLLABLE BEFORE THE SUFFIX IS ACCENTED;
THE SYLLABLE CONTAINS ONLY 1 VOWEL & 1 ENDING CONSONANT;
THE SUFFIX BEGINS WITH A VOWEL.

<u>YES</u>!	<u>NO</u>!
BEGIN & <u>ING</u> = BEGINNING	OFFER & <u>ED</u> = OFFERED
REFER & <u>AL</u> = REFERRAL	RESENT & <u>FUL</u> = RESENTFUL
EQUIP & <u>ED</u> = EQUIPPED	REVEAL & <u>ING</u> = REVEALING

DOUBLING STRATEGY PART 3

BE A SUPER HERO!

PROTECT ANY SINGLE VOWEL
IN DANGER OF LOSING ITS SOUND
BY ADDING ANOTHER CONSONANT.

AT THE BEGINNING OF A WORD: AS SIST, AT TEND	DOUBLE S SS	DOUBLE T TT
DOUBLE M MM	IN THE MIDDLE OF A WORD: COM MAND, SUG GEST	DOUBLE G GG
DOUBLE N NN	DOUBLE P PP	AT THE END OF A WORD: RUN NING, SKIP PED

DOUBLE AT THE END OF A MULTISYLLABIC WORD
IF
THE ACCENTED SYLLABLE COMES BEFORE THE SUFFIX.

DOUBLE THE ENDING CONSONANT IN THE FOLLOWING:

DEFERRED, PROPELLED, REGRETTED.

DON'T DOUBLE THE ENDING CONSONANT IN THE
FOLLOWING WORDS BECAUSE
THE FIRST SYLLABLE IS ACCENTED:

OFFERED, OPENING, EQUALED.

THE DOUBLING STRATEGY

COMBINE EACH ROOT WORD WITH ITS SUFFIX.

1 DOT + ING =

2 CLIP + ER =

3 CAP + FUL =

4 CAP + ED =

5 SLIM + ER =

6 SLIM + NESS =

7 FIT + NESS =

8 FIT + EST =

9 CRAP + Y =

10 CAMP + ER =

11 SAIL + OR =

12 WET + ER =

13 CLAP + ING =

14 STAMP + ING =

15 BOIL + ED =

PRACTICE YOUR SPELLING STRATEGIES:

THE DOUBLING STRATEGY

COMBINE EACH ROOT WORD WITH ITS SUFFIX.

1 RIP + ED   =

2 TRAP + ER   =

3 FLOAT + ING   =

4 NAP + LESS   =

5 TRIP + ED   =

6 PEP + Y   =

7 FOIL + ED   =

8 PLAN + ING   =

9 BAT + MAN   =

10 BAT + ER   =

11 BUG + Y   =

12 RAP + TURE   =

13 RAP + ED   =

14 LAND + ING   =

15 SPOON + FUL   =

ENDING Y MAKES 2 SOUNDS: E AND I

ENDING Y MAKES AN E SOUND IN MOST WORDS WITH MORE THAN 1 VOWEL SOUND.

WEND<u>Y</u> INDUSTR<u>Y</u> EMERGENC<u>Y</u> PROFESSIONALL<u>Y</u>

SUFFIXES THAT END IN Y:		
	SHADY	Y
	VACANCY	CY
	QUICKLY	LY
	SAFETY	TY
	DICTIONARY	ARY
	HUMANITY	ITY
	OBSERVATORY	ORY
	ECOLOGY	OLOGY

THOUSANDS OF WORDS END IN A CONSONANT BEFORE Y.

ENDING Y MAKES AN I SOUND IN A FEW DIFFERENT GROUPS OF WORDS PLUS OCCASIONAL OTHERS.

Y = I AT THE END OF A 1 SYLLABLE WORD.	ENDING Y = I TO FORM THE SUFFIX, FY.	ENDING Y = I AS PART OF THE ROOT, PLY.
TRY DRY FLY MY 	DIGNIFY HORRIFY GRATIFY AMPLIFY 	APPLY REPLY COMPLY MULTIPLY $\begin{array}{r} 2 \\ \times\,4 \\ \hline 8 \end{array}$

TO AVOID MAKING THOUSANDS OF SPELLING ERRORS, DON'T YOU WANT TO MASTER THE CONSONANT Y SPELLING STRATEGY?

CONSONANT Y SPELLING STRATEGY:
TO SWAP OR EXCHANGE OR TRADE!

ROOT WORDS THAT END WITH A CONSONANT BEFORE Y MUST SWAP OR EXCHANGE OR TRADE THE Y FOR AN I BEORE ADDING A SUFFIX.

SURPRISE!
THE I RETAINS THE E SOUND.

CRAZY	VARY	FAMILY
CRAZIER	VARIOUS	FAMILIAL
CRAZIEST	VARIATION	FAMILIAR
CRAZIES	VARIENCE	FAMILIARIZE
CRAZINESS	VARIABLE	FAMILIARITY

BUT... IF THE Y MADE AN I SOUND IN THE ROOT WORD, THEN I KEEPS ITS I SOUND.

DENY	SUPPLY	APPLY
DENIAL	SUPPLIES	APPLIANCE
DENIABLE	SUPPLIED	APPLIABLE
DENIED	SUPPLIER	APPLIED
DENIES	SUPPLIABLE	APPLIES

HOWEVER,
DON'T CHANGE THE Y TO I *IF* Y HAS FORMED A VOWEL TEAM LIKE: PLAYER, KEYS, BOYISH, BUYER

OR IF THE SUFFIX BEGINS WITH THE LETTER I LIKE: COPYING, COPYIST, BABYISH

1 SPY + ED =

2 SPY + ING =

3 HAPPY + LY =

4 HAPPY + EST =

5 DENY + AL =

6 COPY + IST =

7 PAY + ABLE =

8 PAY + MENT =

9 READY + NESS =

10 TERRIFY + ING =

11 GLORY + OUS =

12 JOY + FUL =

13 STEADY + LY =

14 COPY + ES =

15 DUTY + FUL =

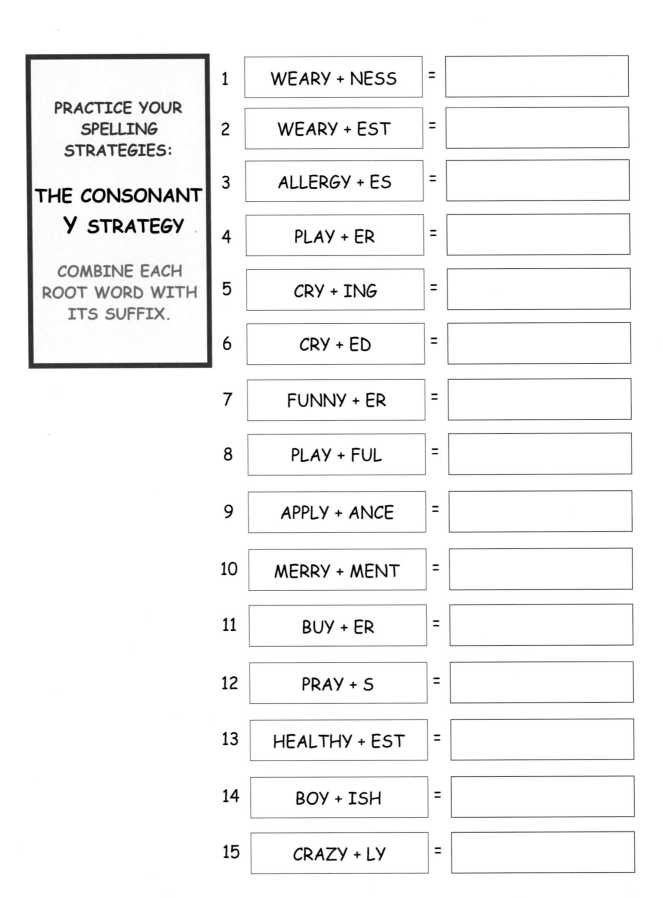

PRACTICE YOUR
SPELLING
STRATEGIES:

**THE CONSONANT
Y STRATEGY**

COMBINE EACH
ROOT WORD WITH
ITS SUFFIX.

1   WEARY + NESS   =
2   WEARY + EST   =
3   ALLERGY + ES   =
4   PLAY + ER   =
5   CRY + ING   =
6   CRY + ED   =
7   FUNNY + ER   =
8   PLAY + FUL   =
9   APPLY + ANCE   =
10 MERRY + MENT   =
11 BUY + ER   =
12 PRAY + S   =
13 HEALTHY + EST =
14 BOY + ISH   =
15 CRAZY + LY   =

WHY E ENDS SO MANY WORDS

VCE
1 VOWEL, 1 CONSONANT, 1 ENDING SILENT E

A VCE SYLLABLE NEEDS ENDING SILENT E TO MAKE ITS OTHER VOWEL SAY ITS NAME IN THE ALPHABET.

ABE LIKES JUNE'S SMILE.

CE
ENDING CE NEEDS E TO CHANGE THE C INTO AN S SOUND.

IN FRANCE, THEY LIKE TO DANCE.

GE
ENDING GE NEEDS E TO CHANGE THE G INTO A J SOUND.

GEORGE WILL EAT AN ORANGE.

VSV
ENDING VOWEL & S & E NEED E TO CHANGE THE S INTO A Z SOUND:
VOWEL S VOWEL = Z

BECAUSE OF A RAISE,
SHE CHOSE A NEW CAR.

ENDING CON. LE
A CON. LE ENDING SYLLABLE CONSISTS OF AN INITIAL CONSONANT THAT VARIES WITH AN LE THAT STAYS.

A CIR CLE OF
GOLD SPAR KLES

+E

SILENT E SPELLING STRATEGY: KEEP OR SUBTRACT THE ENDING SILENT E?

-E

KEEP ENDING SILENT E TO PROTECT THE VOWEL'S RIGHT TO SAY ITS NAME BEFORE A SUFFIX.

IN A VCE SYLLABLE, THE ENDING E FORCES THE OTHER VOWEL TO SAY ITS NAME.

KEEP ENDING SILENT E

+E
- SAFETY
- GENES
- LIVELY
- HOMELESS
- TUNEFUL

BE CONSISTENT & KEEP E

+E
- SENSELESS
- INTENSELY
- ARRANGEMENT
- PEACEFUL

SUBTRACT OR TRASH THE ENDING SILENT E BEFORE ADDING A SUFFIX THAT BEGINS WITH A VOWEL.

WHY? IF THE E COMBINES WITH ANOTHER VOWEL, IT OFTEN CREATES A DIFFERENT, DESTRUCTIVE SOUND.

CORRECT SPELLINGS

-E
- SAVED
- SAVING
- SKATER
- HOPING
- HOPED

INCORRECT SPELLINGS

- SA VEED (SOUNDS LIKE VEDE)
- SA VEING (SOUNDS LIKE VANG)
- SKA TEER (SOUNDS LIKE TEAR)
- HO PEING (SOUNDS LIKE PANG)
- HO PEED (SOUNDS LIKE PEDE)

TO AVOID MAKING THOUSANDS OF SPELLING ERRORS, DON'T YOU WANT TO MASTER THE SILENT E SPELLING STRATEGY?

PRACTICE YOUR SPELLING STRATEGIES:

SILENT E SPELLING STRATEGY

COMBINE EACH ROOT WORD WITH ITS SUFFIX.

#		
1	NICE + LY	=
2	NICE + ER	=
3	SERVE + ING	=
4	TERRIBLE + LY	=
5	TIME + LESS	=
6	HATE + FUL	=
7	SPACE + ING	=
8	COMPETE + ED	=
9	FLAKE + S	=
10	RAISE + ING	=
11	SLICE + ED	=
12	PIMPLE + S	=
13	SAME + NESS	=
14	ICE + ING	=
15	SPICE + Y	=

1   FACE + LESS   =

2   FACE + ED   =

3   STATE + ING   =

4   STATE + MENT   =

5   PRICE + Y   =

6   PRICE + LESS   =

7   TURTLE + S   =

8   BURGLE + AR   =

9   TENSE + ED   =

10   TENSE + NESS   =

11   CARVE + ER   =

12   RACE + ING   =

13   FAME + OUS   =

14   GRATE + FUL   =

15   GRATE + ING   =

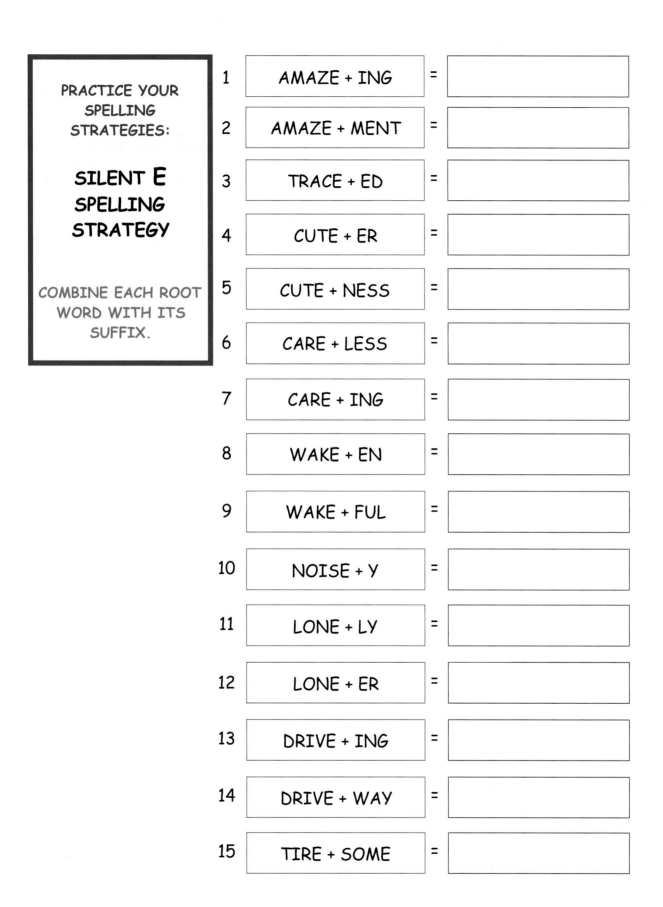

PRACTICE YOUR SPELLING STRATEGIES:

SILENT E SPELLING STRATEGY

COMBINE EACH ROOT WORD WITH ITS SUFFIX.

1 AMAZE + ING =
2 AMAZE + MENT =
3 TRACE + ED =
4 CUTE + ER =
5 CUTE + NESS =
6 CARE + LESS =
7 CARE + ING =
8 WAKE + EN =
9 WAKE + FUL =
10 NOISE + Y =
11 LONE + LY =
12 LONE + ER =
13 DRIVE + ING =
14 DRIVE + WAY =
15 TIRE + SOME =

HOW ROOT WORD ENDS	ACTION	EXAMPLES
— SILENT E SPELLING STRATEGY ROOT WORDS ENDING IN SILENT E	**SUBTRACT E** BEFORE SUFFIXES THAT BEGIN WITH A VOWEL. **KEEP E** BEFORE SUFFIXES THAT BEGIN WITH A CONSONANT.	SKATED SKATER SKATING CAREFUL CARELESS NINETY NICELY
CONSONANT Y SPELLING STRATEGY ROOT WORDS ENDING IN CONSONANT Y	**TRADE** OR **SWAP** Y FOR AN **I** BEFORE SUFFIXES EXCEPT THE **I** STARTING ONES LIKE **ING** AND **IST.**	BABIES BABIED BABYISH
+ **THE DOUBLING STRATEGY**	IF 1 VOWEL IS AT RISK OF LOSING ITS VOWEL SOUND, *DOUBLE THE ENDING CONSONANT BEFORE ADDING THE SUFFIX.*	FITTEST BEGGAR BETTING SOBBED
FOR ROOTS ENDING IN ONLY 1 VOWEL & ONLY 1 CONSONANT	IF A ROOT WORD CONTAINS A VOWEL TEAM, *DO NOT DOUBLE.*	RAINING LOOKED
	IF A ROOT WORD CONTAINS 2 ENDING CONSONANTS, *DO NOT DOUBLE.*	LANDING MASKED *CAN SHARE THE CONSONANTS*
BUT MOST WORDS DO **NOT** NEED TO DOUBLE!	IF A ROOT WORD WITH 1 VOWEL & 1 ENDING CONSONANT ADDS A SUFFIX THAT BEGINS WITH A CONSONANT, *DO NOT DOUBLE.*	FITNESS CANFUL *CAN SHARE THE CONSONANTS*

1	EMPLOY + ER	=	
2	GALLERY + ES	=	
3	WASTE + FUL	=	
4	CLASS + Y	=	
5	SHINE + Y	=	
6	REVIVE + AL	=	
7	SHAPE + LY	=	
8	ENJOY + ABLE	=	
9	GLASSY + NESS	=	
10	READY + LY	=	
11	HASTE + Y	=	
12	TICKLE + ED	=	
13	SQUIRM + ED	=	
14	SET + ING	=	
15	LIE + AR	=	
16	LIKE + ABLE	=	
17	CLAM + Y	=	
18	COMPLY + ANCE	=	
19	REFUSE + AL	=	
20	TRAP + ER	=	

1. CARRY + ED =

2. FINE + AL =

3. TWIRL + ED =

4. OBEY + S =

5. PITY + FUL =

6. NINE + TY =

7. DRIP + ING =

8. SORRY + EST =

9. SHADE + Y =

10. SHIN + ING =

11. PLACE + MENT =

12. EASY + LY =

13. AVOID + ANCE =

14. SCAR + ED =

15. EMPTY + ING =

16. DISMAY + ED =

17. SANE + ITY =

18. GRIT + ING =

19. SLICE + ED =

20. FAT + NESS =

1 PRAY + ING =
2 SWET + ING =
3 DIVE + ING =
4 CRAFTY + LY =
5 WORK + MAN =
6 SPACE + SHIP =
7 MESSY + EST =
8 FIFTY + ES =
9 SERVE + ED =
10 CLIP + ING =
11 PAVE + MENT =
12 GLIDE + ER =
13 WIN + ER =
14 WIN + SOME =
15 SLANT + ED =
16 LIKE + EN =
17 LIKE + LY =
18 FUNNY + ER =
19 CREEP + Y =
20 FLY + ING =

ENDING SPELLING STRATEGY FOR 1 SYLLABLE WORDS

STAFF

FRIENDLESS LETTER **F** NEEDS A TWIN LETTER TO BE HAPPY.

| STA<u>FF</u> | JE<u>FF</u> | TI<u>FF</u> | SCO<u>FF</u> | STU<u>FF</u> |

<u>JEFF</u>'S <u>STAFF</u> WILL <u>SCOFF</u> AT A <u>TIFF</u> OVER SUCH SILLY <u>STUFF</u>.

LONELY LETTER **L** NEEDS A TWIN LETTER TO BE HAPPY.

| TALL | TELL | WILL | DOLL | DULL |

THE <u>TALL</u> BUT <u>DULL</u> <u>DOLL</u> <u>WILL</u> <u>TELL</u> A SECRET.

SAD LETTER **S** NEEDS A TWIN LETTER TO BE HAPPY.

| MA<u>SS</u> | ME<u>SS</u> | MI<u>SS</u> | MO<u>SS</u> | MU<u>SS</u> |

<u>MISS</u> <u>MOSS</u> DOES NOT <u>MESS</u> HER <u>DRESS</u> OR <u>MUSS</u> HER HAIR BEFORE <u>MASS</u>.

ANSWERS TO SPELLING PRACTICES

ANSWERS TO PAGE 13

CLICK	CLUTCH	PLEDGE
SEEK	SNATCH	WAGE
MILK	WITCH	MARGE
LOCK	SKETCH	DREDGE
STACK	PEACH	BADGE
TRUNK	PERCH	FORGE
DECK	PORCH	DIRGE
STORK	LUNCH	JUDGE
SILK	BIRCH	MERGE
STUCK	MARCH	BRIDGE
PARK	BEACH	CHARGE
PUCK	BUTCH	LODGE
TRACK	DUTCH	PURGE
WORK	TORCH	BARGE
KICK	MITCH	EDGE

ANSWERS TO PAGE 14

BLEAK	LAUNCH	BUDGE
FLICK	POUCH	LEDGE
TICK	REACH	SCROOGE
KNOCK	FRENCH	FUDGE
HIKE	CRUTCH	FRINGE
SNUCK	SWITCH	SMIDGE
CRACK	NOTCH	OBLIGE
HOOK	STRETCH	RIDGE
FORK	ARCH	HUGE
RAKE	HATCH	SPLURGE
HAWK	BENCH	WEDGE
SMIRK	DRENCH	ORANGE
STARK	INCH	STAGE
WEEK	REACH	SLUDGE
THICK	BATCH	LARGE

PAGE 25 / PAGE 26

PAGE 25	PAGE 26
DOTTING	RIPPED
CLIPPER	TRAPPER
CAPFUL	FLOATING
CAPPED	NAPLESS
SLIMMER	TRIPPED
SLIMNESS	PEPPY
FITNESS	FOILED
CRAPPY	PLANNING
CAMPER	BATMAN
SAILOR	BUGGY
WETTER	RAPTURE
CLAPPING	RAPPED
STAMPING	LANDING
BOILED	SPOONFUL

PAGE 29 / PAGE 30

PAGE 29	PAGE 30
SPIED	WEARINESS
SPYING	WEARIEST
HAPPILY	ALLERGIES
HAPPIEST	PLAYER
DENIAL	CRYING
COPYIST	CRIED
PAYABLE	FUNNIER
PAYMENT	PLAYFUL
READINESS	APPLIANCE
TERRIFYING	MERRIMENT
GLORIOUS	BUYER
JOPYFUL	PRAYS
STEADILY	HEALTHIEST
COPIES	BOYISH
DUTIFUL	CRAZILY

ANSWERS TO SPELLING PRACTICES

PAGE 33

NICELY
NICER
SERVING
TERRIBLY
TIMELESS
HATEFUL
SPACING
COMPETED
FLAKES
RAISING
SLICED
PIMPLES
SAMENESS
ICING
SPICY

PAGE 34

FACELESS
FACED
STATING
STATEMENT
PRICY
PRICELESS
TURTLES
BURGLAR
TENSED
TENSENESS
CARVER
RACING
FAMOUS
GRATEFUL
GRATING

PAGE 35

AMAZING
AMAZEMENT
TRACED
CUTER
CUTENESS
CARELESS
CARING
WAKEN
WAKEFUL
NOISY
LONELY
LONER
DRIVER
DRIVEWAY
TIRESOME

PAGE 37

EMPLOYER
GALLERIES
WASTEFUL
CLASSY
SHINY
REVIVAL
SHAPELY
ENJOYABLE
GLASSINESS
READILY
HASTY
TICKLED
SQUIRMED
SETTING
LIAR
LIKABLE
CLAMMY
COMPLIANCE
REFUSAL
TRAPPER

PAGE 38

CARRIED
FINAL
TWIRLED
OBEYS
PITIFUL
NINETY
DRIPPING
SORRIEST
SHADY
SHINNING
PLACEMENT
EASILY
AVOIDANCE
SCARRED
EMPTYING
DISMAYED
SANITY
GRITTING
SLICED
FATNESS

PAGE 39

PRAYING
SWETTING
DIVING
CRAFTILY
WORKMAN
SPACESHIP
MESSIEST
FIFTIES
SERVED
CLIPPING
PAVEMENT
GLIDER
WINNER
WINSOME
SLANTED
LIKEN
LIKELY
FUNNIER
CREEPY
FLYING

Made in United States
Orlando, FL
13 March 2023

31000456R00029